COLIN MATTHEWS

Palinode

for solo cello

(1992)

Palinode was commissioned by Pamela Hind O'Malley and the
Eastern Arts Board, and first performed by Pamela Hind O'Malley
in St Edward's Church, Cambridge, on 29 July 1992,
as part of the 1992 Cambridge Arts Festival

Duration: 10 minutes

PROGRAMME NOTE

A Palinode is, in poetry, a recantation, or more simply, second thoughts. The term applies twice over to this work, since in the first place it reflects the fact that, having set out to write a series of short studies for solo cello, I became distracted by a study in slow tempo, and this became - contrary to my original intention - the basis of the whole piece. But it also relates to the contrast between this work and my orchestral piece *Broken Symmetry*, completed a week or so before I began work on *Palinode*, and whose 200 pages of hectic activity last only just over twice the length of the four pages of this score. *Palinode* consists, in effect, of a sequence of variations on the opening melody, rising gradually to a climax which quite quickly dies away.

C.M.

PALINODE

Solo Cello

Colin Matthews

4

* Make the transition into longer note-values as imperceptible as possible.

February–March 1992